CONTEMPORARY
WEDDING
CAKES

NADENE HURST
JULIE SPRINGALL

MEREHURST

Contents

Introduction 6

Authors' dedications

*My contribution to this book is dedicated to my
husband, Bruce, who is my constant source of
love, help and support. My grateful thanks to
Kathleen for her help with the flowers. XH*

*Dedicated to my husband, Mikey, thanks for
your love, encouragement, constructive criticism
and for reworking my templates; also to Chloe,
our chocolate cake baker and tester. JS*

Royal-iced wedding cakes

Royal icing is the traditional form of decoration used
for wedding cakes and cakes created for special occasions.
Its flat surface and delicate finish creates a very versatile
style, which is of great beauty and elegance when executed
to a good standard. The cakes in this section reflect a variety
of the techniques possible with this classical medium, while
representing an up-to-date approach to cake design.